SONGS OF IMPERFECTION

Poetry by Stanley Moss

THE WRONG ANGEL

SKULL OF ADAM

THE INTELLIGENCE OF CLOUDS

ASLEEP IN THE GARDEN

A HISTORY OF COLOR

STANLEY MOSS

Songs
of
Imperfection

ANVIL PRESS POETRY

Published in 2004
by Anvil Press Poetry Ltd
Neptune House 70 Royal Hill London SE10 8RF
www.anvilpresspoetry.com

This book is published with financial assistance
from Arts Council England

Designed and set in Monotype Bembo by Anvil
Printed and bound in England
by Cromwell Press, Trowbridge, Wiltshire

ISBN 0 85646 366 3

A catalogue record for this book
is available from the British Library

For Peter

ACKNOWLEDGMENTS

The American Poetry Review, PN Review (UK), *Poetry,*
The New Yorker, The Times Literary Supplement, Poetry London,
The New York Times, The Nation, Partisan Review, Pequod, Parnassus,
Best Poems of 2003, The New Republic, The Forward Book of Poetry
2004, Dissent, Exile, Tikkun, Verse, Exquisite Corpse, Poetry
International, Princeton University Library Chronicle, Slate.

CONTENTS

God is the sole being who has no need to exist in order to reign.

BAUDELAIRE

A HISTORY OF COLOR

I

What is heaven but the history of color,
dyes washed out of laundry, cloth and cloud,
mystical rouge, lipstick, eye shadows? Harlot nature,
explain the color of tongue, lips, nipples,
against Death come ons of labia, penis, the anus,
the concupiscent color wheels of insects and birds,
explain why Christian gold and blue tempt the kneeling,
why Moslem green is miraculous in the desert,
why the personification of the rainbow is Iris,
the mother of Eros, why *Adam* in Hebrew
comes out of the redness of earth . . .
The cosmos and impatiens I planted this June
may outlast me, these yellow, pink and blue annuals
do not sell indulgences, a rose ravishes a rose.
The silver and purple pollen that has blown on the roof
of my car concludes a sacred conversation.

Against Death washerwomen and philosophers
sought a fixative for colors to replace unstable substances
like saliva, urine and blood, the long process of boiling
washing and rinsing. It is Death who works
with clean hands and a pure heart. Against him
Phoenician red-purple dyes taken from sea snails, the colors
fixed by exposing wool to air of the morning seas near Sidon,
or the sunlight and winds on the limestone cliffs of Crete—
all lost, which explains a limestone coastline
changed into mountains of pink-veined marble,
the discarded bodies of gods.
Of course Phoenician purple made for gods
and heroes cannot be produced nowadays.
Virgil thought purple was the color of the soul—

all lost. Anyone can see the arithmetic when purple
was pegged to the quantity and price of seashells.

Remember
the common gray and white seagull looked down
at the Roman Republic, at the brick-red and terracotta
dominant after the pale yellow stone of the Greek world,
into the glare of the Empire's white marble.
The sapphire and onyx housefly that circled
the jeweled crowns of Byzantium buzzed prayers,
thinks what it thinks, survives. Under a Greek sky
the churches held Christ alive to supplicants,
a dove alighted on a hand torn by nails.
In holy light and darkness
the presence of Christ is cupped in silver.
Death holds, whether you believe Christ
is there before you or not, you will not see Him later—
sooner prick the night sky with a needle to find the moon.

2

I fight Death with peppermints, a sweet to recall
the Dark Ages before the word *orange* existed.
In illuminated manuscripts St. Jerome,
his robes *egg-red*, is seen translating in the desert,
a golden lion at his feet—
or he is tied to a column naked in a dream,
flagellated for reading satires and Pliny's
Natural History that describes
the colors used by Apelles, the Greek master,
in a painting of grapes so true to life
birds would alight on them to feed.
Death, you tourist, you've seen it all and better before,
your taste: whipped saints sucking chastity's thumb,
while you eat your candy of diseased and undernourished infants.

On an afternoon when death seemed no more than a newspaper
in a language I could not read, I remember
looking down at Jerusalem from the Mount of Olives,
that my friend said:"Jerusalem is a harlot,
everyone who passes leaves a gift."
Do birds of prey sing madrigals?
Outside the walls of Jerusalem, the crusaders
dumped mounds of dead Muslims
and their green banners, the severed heads of Jews,
some still wrapped in prayer shawls,
while the Christian dead sprawled near the place of a skull
which is called in Hebrew *Golgotha.*
Among the living, blood and blood-soaked prayers,
on the land of God's broken promises—a flagged javelin
stuck into the Holy Sepulcher as into a wild boar.

Hauled back by the "Franks", colors never seen in Europe,
wonders of Islam, taffetas, organdies, brocades, damasks.
Gold-threaded cloth that seemed made for the Queen of Heaven
was copied in Italy on certain paintings of Our Lady,
on her blue robes in gold in Arabic:
"There is no God but God, Muhammad is His Prophet"—
for whom but Death to read?
Wrapped in a looted prayer rug,
an idea seized by Aquinas: the separation of faith and reason.
Later nicked from the library of Baghdad:
the invention of paper brought from China
by pilgrims on a hajj, looted rhyme, lenses,
notes on removing cataracts.
Certain veils would be lifted from the eyes of Europe,
all only for Death to see.
Within sight of Giotto's white, green and pink marble bell-tower
that sounded the promise of Paradise,
plants and insects were used for dyes made from oak gall,
bastard saffron, beetle, canary weed, cockroach,

the fixative was fermented piss from a young boy
or a man drunk on red wine, while the painters
mixed their pigments with egg yolks and albumen,
gold with lime, garlic, wax and casein
that dried hard as adamantine, buffed with a polished agate
or a wolf's tooth.

At the time of the Plague, while the dead
lay unattended in the streets of Europe,
the yellow flag hung out more often than washing,
someone cloistered wrote a text
on making red from cinnabar, saffron from crocus,
each page an illuminated example.
At the Last Supper the disciples sat dead at table.
Still, by the late fifteenth century
color was seen as ornament,
almost parallel to the colors of rhetoric,
blue was moving away from its place describing
the vaults of heaven to the changing sky of everyday.
Does it matter to heaven if a sleeve is blue or red or black?
In Venice Titian found adding lead-white to azurite-blue
changed a blue sleeve to satin.

3

I think the absence of color is like a life without love.
A master can draw every passion with a pencil, but light,
shadow and dark cannot reveal the lavender iris
between the opened thighs of a girl still almost a child,
or, before life was through with her, the red and purple
pomegranate at the center of her being.

Against Death on an English day Newton discovered
a single ray of white light refracted,
decomposed into a spectrum of colors,

and that he could reconstruct the totality,
mischievously reverse the process,
then produce white light again—which perhaps is why
last century, in a painting by Max Ernst,
the Holy Mother is spanking the baby Jesus.

Goethe found a like proof on a sunny summer day—
the birds, I suppose, as usual devouring insects
courting to the last moment of life.
While sitting by a crystal pool watching
soldiers fishing for trout, the poet was taken
by spectrums of color refracted from a ceramic shard
at the bottom of the pool, then from the tails of swimming trout
catching fire and disappearing,
until a rush of thirsty horses, tired and dirtied by war,
muddied the waters.

A heroic tenor sings to the exploding sun:
"Every war is a new dawning"—Fascist music.
Death would etch Saturn devouring his children on coins
if someone would take his money.
Of course his IOU is good as gold.

Turner had sailors lash him to the mast
to see into a storm, then he painted slavers
throwing overboard the dead and dying,
sharks swimming through shades of red.
He painted the atheist Avalanche, then heaven
in truthful colors: Rain, Steam, Speed.
"Portraits of nothing and very like," they said, "tinted steam."
Turner kept most of his paintings to leave to England,
his Burning of the Houses of Parliament.

Against oblivion a still life of two red apples
stands for a beautiful woman. On her shoulder

the bruise of a painter's brush—she is no more
than a still life of peasant shoes.
"You will not keep apples or shoes or France," Death says.
A child chooses an object first for color,
then for form, in rooms with mother, father,
Death, and all the relatives of being.

4

Now this coloratura moves off-stage
to the present, which is a kind of intermission.
My friend Mark Rothko painted a last canvas,
gray and yellow, then took a kitchen knife, half cut off his wrists
bound and knotted behind his back
(a trick of the mind Houdini never mastered)
to throw off Eros, who rode his back and whipped him
even after he was dead, till Eros, the little Greek,
was covered with blood of the Song of Songs.
Now Rothko is a study of color, a purple chapel,
a still river where he looks for his mother and father.

Death, you tourist with too much luggage,
you can distinguish the living from your dead.
Can you tell Poseidon's trident from a cake fork,
the living from the living,
winter from summer, autumn from spring?
In a sunless world, even bats nurse their young,
hang upside down looking for heaven,
make love in a world where the lion, afraid of no beast,
runs in terror from a white chicken. Such are your winnings.
Death, I think you take your greatest pleasure
in watching us murdering in great numbers
in ways even you have not planned.
They say in paradise every third thought is of earth
and a woman with a child at her breast.

TO MY FRIEND BORN BLIND

You told me your blindness is not seeing
even the shades of black called darkness.
You felt useless as a mirror until you made a poem
useful as a dog with bells around its neck.
Sometimes you wake to the wind moving through different trees.
A child, you loved to touch your mother's face,
you wished the world were ocean,
you could hear, smell, and taste knew that it was blue.
Trees had a smell you called green, apples red.
How could the flag be red-white-and-blue?
You laugh when I tell you "Drink to me only with thine eyes"
is a love song, that some who see
only make love in the dark. You wish you could see as a bat.
Mozart you say is the great equalizer, the truest democrat.
You always preferred a dog to a cane.
When in Braille you first read, "the disciples asked,
'Rabbi, who sinned: this man or his parents that he was born blind?'
Jesus answering, 'Neither hath this man sinned nor his parents,
but that the works of God should be revealed in him . . .'
and he spat on the ground and healed the man
with his spit and mud—" you waited awhile, then read on.
Blind in dreams, you touch, taste, smell and hear—
see nothing, nightmares like crowds are the more terrible
because you never see what terrifies you.
Since childhood it was an act of faith
to believe the sun and moon were in the sky,
it pleased you the sun is a fire the sighted cannot look into . . .
It is late. As always you, my imaginary friend,
take me by the hand and lead me to bed.

IMPERFECTION

Whom can I tell? Who cares?
I see the shell of a snail protected by a flaw
in its design: white is time, blue-green is rot,
something emerging in the rough dust, the unused
part of a shape that is furious and calm.
In aging grasses, knotted with their being,
the snail draws near the east bank of the pond,
not because that is where the morning sun is,
but out of coastal preference, raising
a tawny knotted counterwhirl
like a lion cub against its mother's haunch,
anus of a star. But let the conch stand
in the warm mud, with its horn become an eye,
suffering the passion of any snail:
a hopeful birth, a death, an empty tomb.
I'd walk with this horned eye, lip-foot after lip-foot,
beyond the dry wall of my life, backward
into the sacramental mud, where the soul begins to reason—
as on that afternoon Aristotle dissecting
squid proclaimed "the eternity of the world."
There is not a thing on earth without a star
that beats upon it and tells it to grow.

SUBWAY TOKEN

If Walt Whitman were alive and young and still living in Brooklyn,
he would have seen the burning Trade Center,
and if he were old and still in Camden, New Jersey,
he would have seen men jumping out from a hundred stories up,
some holding hands, believers and nonbelievers
who prefer a leap of faith to a death in an ocean of fire.
Walt could have seen women falling from the sun,
although the sun has no offices.
True, in the heavens there often has been a kind of tit for tat,
not just thunder for lightning:
where there is grandeur observed, something human, trivial.

The South Tower fell like the old Whitman
although it was second to be struck,
then the North Tower like the young Whitman.
What history, what hallucination?
Anyone could see the towers fell like the great poet,
with three thousand people from eighty-seven countries,
and three hundred and forty-three firefighters
into the irrational fires that burned for ninety days.
None of these persons lived in boarding houses
as would be likely in Whitman's time.
History, hallucination?
A life goes up in flame like a page of bible paper.
You could not pile books so high, not good books,
as this grand canyon of steel and concrete body parts,
my city's broken backbone pushed out through his throat.

THE BLANKET

The man who never prays
accepts that the wheat field in summer
kneels in prayer when the wind blows across it,
that the wordless rain and snow
protect the world from blasphemy.
His wife covers him with a blanket
on a cold night—it is, perhaps, a prayer?
The man who never prays says kindness and prayer
are close, but not as close as sleep and death.
He does not observe the Days of Awe,
all days are equally holy to him.
In late September, he goes swimming
in the ocean, surrounded by divine intervention.

THE FALCON

My son carries my ghost on his shoulder, a falcon,
I am careful not to dig in my claws. I play
I am his father owl, sometimes sparrow, a hummingbird
in his ear. I told him from my first chirp:
"Be an American democratic Jew mensch-bird."
When he was a child in Italy I was a migrant bird
with a nest in America. When I flew home
he cried "*Perche, perche?*" I wept
not wanting him to have a distant bird
or a sea captain for a father.
How many times did I cross the Atlantic
in the worst weather to perch outside his window?
What kind of nest could I make in Italy
on a hotel balcony? When he needed to be held
his mother and nannies held him. When he reached out
to me he often fell. He said *I know I know* to everything
I might have taught him. I fought for his life
with one wing tied behind my back—
for his name, school, and to have his hair cut
in a man's barber shop, not a salon for signoras.
"Lose to him! Lose to him!" his mother screamed.
I was the only one in his life
who would not throw a footrace
he could win in a year, fair and square.
How could a small boy spend so much time
laughing and talking to a father in restaurants?
He complained in Bologna I took him to six museums,
in Florence four, in Espagna *mille e tre.*
We laughed at those rare Italian birds
who don't find themselves sleeping forever
on a bed of polenta—preening, displaying,
making a *bella figura.* An omen in his life.

I flew him to an English meadow
to study Dante, then Shakespeare's histories
in a king maple overlooking the Hudson,
the cast: himself, me, my mate the beautiful Jane bird.

What are years? Not a herd of cattle,
perhaps a flock of birds passing overhead.
Sometimes I hear him chirping my song
louder than I ever sang it.
One day, when the heavenly dogs and hell dogs
find me behind a bush and fight over me,
may one with a soft mouth break from the pack
and take most of me to his Master. Let Him say, "Good dog,
good dog, what a peculiar kind of bird is this,
with his gray curly feathers and strange beak?
Have I ever heard him sing?" May it dawn upon Him,
I am the bird with the good son.

BABIES

Babies, babies,
before you can see more than light or darkness,
before your mothers have kissed your heads,
I come to you with news of dead and dying friends.
You, so close to the miracle of life,
lend me a miracle to bring to my friend.
Babies, babies.
Once Death was a baby, he grasped God's little finger
to keep from falling—kicking and chortling
on his back, unbaptized, uncircumcised,
but invited to share sunlight and darkness
with the rest of us. Mother Death would nurse him,
comfort and wash him when he soiled himself
in the arms of the mourners and the heartbroken.

Older, Death took his place
at table beside his mother—her "angel."
They ate and drank from each other's mouth and fingers,
laughed at their private jokes. He could play for her
any musical instrument, knew all music by heart,
all birdsong, the purr, growl, snort, or whine
of every animal.
The story goes that, fat with eternal life,
all breath merely brushed and smoothed his wings,
older than his mother, he devoured her,
far from light or darkness.

Babies, at the moment of your first uncertain breath,
when your mother's magic blood is still upon you,
I come to you, the helpless ones still coughing
from miracles of birth.

Babies hardly heavier than clouds,
in desperation, for my friend, for a lark
I hold up the sac you broke through
as if it were *Saint Veronica's Veil*—
but no face is on it, no blood changed to wine,
no blood from marrow.
I hold up a heavy sack of useless words.
I shake a rattle to catch your eye or first smile.

PRAISE

For Yehuda Amichai

I

Snow clouds shadow the bay, on the ice the odd fallen gull.
I try to keep my friend from dying by remembering
his childhood of praise to God, who needs us all. Würzburg:
the grownups are inside saying prayers for the dead,
the children are sent out to play—their laughter
more sacred than prayer. After dark his father
blesses and kisses him *Gutenacht*. He wakes
to go to school with children who stayed behind
and were murdered before promotion.

Now his wife lies beside him.
He may die with her head on his pillow.
He sings in his sleep:
"Her breasts are white sheep that appear on the mountain,
her belly is like a heap of wheat set about with lilies."
Awake, he says, as if telling me a secret:
"When metaphor and reality come together, death occurs."
His life is a light, fresh snow blowing across the bay.

2

A year later in Jerusalem, he carries a fallen soldier
on his back, himself. The text for the day begins:
"He slew a lion in the pit in a time of snow."
Seconds, minutes, hours are flesh,
he tells me he is being cut to pieces—
if they had not made him turn in his rifle . . .
He sees I can not bear more of that.

Yet a little sleep, a little slumber, a little folding
of hands in sleep and we drink *to life*.
Chilled in desert heat, what keeps him alive:
soldiers—his wife, his son and daughter,
perhaps the ashes of a girl he loved in childhood.
Outside their window
a Sun Bird and Dead Sea Sparrow fly
from everlasting to everlasting.
Later he covers my head with his hands, blessing me,
later unable to walk alone he holds onto my hand
with so much strength he comforts me.

CHINESE PRAYER

God of Walls and Ditches, every man's friend,
although you may be banqueting in heaven
on the peaches of immortality
that ripen once every three thousand years,
protect a child I love in China
and on her visits to the United States,
if your powers reach this far, this locality.
You will know her because she is nine years old,
already a beauty and an artist. She needs more
than the natural protection of a tree on a hot day.
You have so many papers,
more than the God of Examinations,
more than the God of Salaries,
who is not for me, because I am self-employed.
It may help you find her to know her mother
was once my bookkeeper,
her brother is a God in the family,
who at six still does not wipe his bottom.
Protect her from feeling worthless.
She is the most silent of children.
She has given me so many drawings and masks,
today I offered her fifty dollars for a painting.
Without a smile she answered,
"How much do you get for a metaphor?"
Sir, here is a little something to keep the incense burning,
remember her to the Almighty God whose character is Jade.

HEART WORK

No moon is as precisely round as the surgeon's light
I see in the center of my heart.
Dangling in a lake of blood, a stainless steel hook,
unbaited, is fishing in my heart for clots.
Across the moon I see a familiar dragonfly,
a certain peace comes of that. Then the dragonfly
gives death or gives birth to a spider it becomes—
they are fishing in my heart with a bare hook,
without a worm—they didn't even fish like that
when the Iroquois owned Manhattan.
Shall I die looking into my heart, seeing so little,
will the table I lie on become a barge, floating
endlessly down river, or a garbage scow?

There is a storm over the lake.
There are night creatures about me:
a Chinese doctor's face I like and a raccoon I like.
I hear a woman reciting numbers growing larger and larger
which I take as bad news—I think I see a turtle,
then on the surface an asp or coral snake.
One bite from a coral snake in Mexico,
you'll take a machete and cut off your arm
if you want to live. I would do that if it would help.

I say, "It's a miracle." The Chinese doctor and the moon
look down on me, and say silently, "Who is this idiot?"
I tell myself, if I lie still enough I'll have a chance,
if I keep my eyes open they will not close forever.
I recall that Muhammad was born from a blood clot.
If I'm smiling, my smile must be like a scissors opening,
a knife is praying to a knife.

Little did I know, in a day, on a Walkman,
I would hear Mozart's second piano concerto,
that I would see a flock of Canada geese flying south
down the East River past the smokestacks of Long Island City.
I had forgotten the beauty in the world. I remember. I remember.

THE LOST BROTHER

I knew that tree was my lost brother
when I heard he was cut down
at four thousand eight hundred sixty-two years;
I knew we had the same mother.
His death pained me. I made up a story.
I realized, when I saw his photograph,
he was an evergreen, a bristlecone like me
who had lived from an early age
with a certain amount of dieback,
at impossible locations, at elevations
over 10,000 feet in extreme weather.
His company: other conifers,
the rosy finch, the rock wren, the raven and clouds,
blue and silver insects that fed mostly off each other.
Some years bighorn sheep visited in summer—
he was entertained by red bats, black-tailed jackrabbits,
horned lizards, the creatures old and young he sheltered.
Beside him in the shade, pink mountain pennyroyal—
to his south, white angelica.
I am prepared to live as long as he did
(it would please our mother),
live with clouds and those I love
suffering with God.
Sooner or later, some bag of wind will cut me down.

PROPHECY

An oracle told me
an elephant in a zoo
will pick up a child
in a red shirt, higher
than he has ever been
in a swing or a see-saw—
the trunk an S
over the elephant's head.
His father will drop
his ice cream cone,
the kid will wave to the world
hello, goodbye—
then swoosh across the moat.
That's the way it will happen.
You will call the mother
saying, "Darling,
I have something to tell you . . ."
the taste of chocolate
still in your mouth.
And you are the father
and you are the child.

CREED

I salute a word, I stand up and give it my chair,
because this one Zulu word, *ubuntu*,
holds what English takes seven to say:
"the essential dignity of every human being."
I give my hand to *ubuntu*—
the simple, everyday South African word
for the English mouthful.
I do not know the black Jerusalems of Africa,
or how to dance its sacred dances.
I can not play Christ's two commandments on the drums:
"Love God" and "Love thy neighbor as thyself."
I do not believe the spirits of the dead
are closer to God than the living,
nor do I completely take to heart
the understanding of *ubuntu*
that teaches reconciliation
of murderers, torturers, accomplices,
with victims still living. I see
it is not blood but *ubuntu*
that is the manure of freedom.

BEAUTY IS NOT EASY

What are they but cattle, these butterflies,
their purple hides torn by barbed wire,
scarred blue, yellow and scarlet.
If they are not marked for slaughter
I cannot tell to whom they belong.
They are just stray cattle.
The sun does not witness,
the clouds do not testify.
Beauty does not need a public defender,
but I would listen to a serious defense
of beauty—tell me what happens to the carcass,
the choice cuts, everything useful:
hide, bones, intestines, fat.
Then talk to me of butterflies.

THE LAST JUDGMENT

Pushing up through a hole in the red marble floor of heaven
a black prisoner sentenced to death
shows his tattooed resurrected flesh:
a blue tear under the outside corners of his eyes,
on his arm two copulating dragons,
their eyes a woman's breasts,
a pierced bleeding heart on his back the size of an eagle,
his chest bears the face of Christ.
Anathema, it cannot be true such unlikely flesh rises to heaven.

Now in the maw of heaven
I see poor losers shrouded with eternal ink—
it's a little like whistling against Bach's B-minor Mass,
there is so much ecclesiastical counterfeit money around:
the anti-Christ silver dollar, the St. Sebastian dime.
Asleep on the marble floor a drowned sailor,
at his knee a cock, his wrists ringed with barbed wire;
a woman walks in circles,
her body still scented with the lilies of death,
her mouth the shape of her lovemaking,
a wolf's head on her shoulder,
its nose nestled between her breasts.
Beneath a huge egg hanging from a cord
a woman who seems to be mad
says she will die if she sleeps alone,
a vine of tiny roses runs down both sides of her belly
to her bush still moist, a large bee put where the hair begins—
on her back, lovers beneath a tree in full foliage
and the motto: *God is the name of my desire.*
Anathema, it cannot be true such unlikely flesh rises to heaven.

Is it true Jewish children with tattooed numbers on their arms
keep their religion even in heaven?
I look at my own flesh with the dyes of age,
the craquelure of love and capriccios. How many nights
have I fallen asleep to the beat of the oars in a boat
with the adult passengers: summer, winter, autumn, spring—
not knowing who is the designer, who the boatman,
the needles writing all night like dreams,
awaking, as all of us, to an uncompleted world,
to the *Behold I am standing before Thy face.*

SONG OF ALPHABETS

When I see Arabic headlines
like the wings of snakebirds,
Persian or Chinese notices
for the arrivals and departures of buses—
information beautiful as flights of starlings—
I cannot tell vowel from consonant,
the signs of the vulnerability of the flesh
from signs for laws and government.

The Hebrew writing on the wall
is all consonants, the vowel
the ache and joy of life
is known by heart. There are words
written in my blood I cannot read.
I can believe a cloud gave us the laws,
parted the Red Sea, gave us the flood,
the rainbow. A cloud teaches kindness,
be prepared for the worst wind, be light of spirit.
Perhaps I have seen His cloud,
an ordinary mongrel cloud
that assumes nothing, demonstrates nothing,
that comforts as a dog sleeping in the room,
a presence offering not salvation
but a little peace.

My hand has touched the ancient Mayan God
whose face is words: a limestone beasthead
of flora, serpent and numbers,
the sockets of a skull I thought were vowels.
Hurrah for English, hidden miracles,
the A and E of waking and sleeping,
the O of mouth.

Thank you, Sir, alone with your name,
for the erect L in love and open-legged V,
beautiful the Tree of Words in the forest
beside the Tree of Souls, lucky the bird
that held Alpha or Omega in his beak.

THE GREAT TREE

It took more than fifty men, women and children
holding hands in a circle to reach around it.
No cloud remembers the flights or kinds of birds
that nested in its branches, how many deer scraped
their antlers against its bark in rutting seasons.
The tree records generations of mountain cats
that sharpened their claws on its trunk, armies of common insects
fighting for a river or a gully in its bark. Looking up
to its crown, it seemed higher than the Brooklyn Bridge
from a ferry passing beneath—some were frightened.
Nothing records the great tree's gentleness with bees
and butterflies, its hospitality to grey squirrels—
that for centuries snakes, toads and horned lizards
nested in its dead branches—
the joy and sorrow of heavy rains and snows,
its heroism at the timberline or its lifelong love of clouds.

Anxious to take the great tree's measure, an "arborist,"
a tree person, chose to count its rings by drilling
with a diamond-tipped corer. Putting his back into the drill,
he quickly passed through American history,
knot and counter-knot, to the age of Mozart,
through the Baroque, through Shakespearian grain,
through a charcoal cave where lightning struck,
through the time of Jesus and Buddha's enlightenment.
In the era of the prophets, the drill broke.
What could a tree person do?
To save his drill, he appealed to a forest ranger,
who with an orange hydraulic saw felled the great tree.

When they counted rings,
they came to four thousand eight hundred sixty-two years.
The tree he killed was the oldest known living thing on earth.

Where can you weep for the tree that had wept and laughed
beyond all human consequence? No one could agree
what poured out: butterflies or troupes of prima ballerinas,
old men or unemployed youths who never found a purpose,
folios, books, leaflets or turtles
with ancient Chinese writing on their backs.
A madman shouted that God had carried the tree to heaven.
Everyone let him rave. Some say the fallen tree began to shudder
and sing a requiem for all the slaughtered, innocent multitudes.
Lingering a moment before they disappeared,
two shadows searched for their young.
Or were they two readers in the Warsaw ghetto
stopping to buy a book out of a discarded baby carriage?

A REFRESHMENT

In our new society, all the old religious orders and titles
are ice creams: Rabbis, Priests, Mullahs,
Gurus, Buddhists, Shiites, Sunni, Dominicans,
Franciscans, Capuchins, Carmelites—ice cream,
never before have the kids had such a choice of flavors,
never before have the Ten Commandments been so cool in summer.
I believe when the holy family rested on their flight to Egypt,
in the desert heat, they had a little mystical lemon or orange ice,
before chocolate and vanilla crossed the unnamed Atlantic.
Let us pray, not for forgiveness, but for our just dessert.

THE FILM CRITIC IMAGINAIRE

He found his good wife weeping alone
when their friend's infidelity was discovered.
She had long pretended her husband's playing around
was like filmmaking: a take here, a take there,
out of sequence, everything but their life together
would end up on the cutting-room floor.
Now she wept at breakfast,
forgot to pick up his suit at the cleaners,
and wept over that.
Angered, he realized his friend's infidelity
had held a full-length mirror to his own,
that the friend's behavior was unacceptable:
he had inconvenienced the distinguished critic,
the reader, the anglophile, the man of the left.
For some days, my life was a fly buzzing around his head—
he swatted with the *Times*.

HOT NEWS, STALE NEWS

Thucydides tells us in an election year
Pisistratus, the Athenian tyrant,
wanting the protection of a god,
got the biggest beautiful woman he could find,
dressed her in silver and gold armor,
proclaimed her the goddess Athena
and drove through the streets of Athens
with the goddess at his side.
In our elections, every candidate
wants to be photographed
going to or coming from Jesus.
One declared "Jesus is in my heart,"
but when he refused to stay
the death warrants for a hundred or so,
his Jesus was silent.

Our presidential candidates
like Roman emperors
favor the death penalty,
but in two thousand years there is a difference.
No candidate would do it for fun, or think death
a competent sentence for cutting down trees
or killing deer, as in 18th-century England.
It's not all blood and circus:
when Camus asked de Gaulle,
"What can a writer do for France?"
the President replied: "Write well!"
Have you heard what's new on the Rialto:
since Pope John Paul declared anti-Semitism a sin
hell has been so crowded
you can't find a decent room there at a hotel.
No one stoops to eloquence.

THE BLACK MAPLE

After an August Atlantic hurricane,
no curled brine-drenched leaf
was at first to Katherine's eye
a Monarch butterfly,
yet she telephoned the news:
flights of deceived Monarchs
had dropped down on her Black Maple
till she could not tell
leaf from butterfly.
In the morning when I arrived
only the tree of metaphor was there,
the butterflies gone to Mexico,
Katherine and her lover, soon to marry,
returned to Manhattan
to practice medicine and music.
Left behind by so much storm and flutter,
I have almost lost count of the seasons.

THE CELESTIAL FOX

I

Death is a celestial fox that leaps out of his coffin.
Tonight his tail sweeps away insects,
which the religious read as a sign:
the fox kills but does not end their lives.
Sometimes he stops, noses the air,
sings, showing his teeth.
I wish I just owed him money.

2

When my two dogs and I run on the beach
innocently thinking we hunt the fox
because we see two eyes in the ocean
where the fox crouches at the foot of a great wave,
my dogs jump in barking at nothing I can see,
while the fox leaps into its true lair,
the moist den of every sexual act.
There he waits, waits with that I–told–you–so grin.

3

I am a great cunt waiting for death to fuck me
between the golden thighs of endless morning,
swaddled in labia. American,
architect of my own destiny,
he shall not flatter me or marry me,
he shall not suck me or finger–fuck me
though I am wet as the Mississippi,
death shall not slip it in.

POST-SURGERY SONG

My surgeon went harrowing like Christ in Hell,
dug a virtuous pagan tumor from my kidney.
"What do I look like inside?" I asked. "Just like every other,
except the distance from your kidney to your heart."
"Aah," I thought, "I have a certain lonely alley inside,
like the Vicolo della Bella Donna in Florence."
I thought I knew the catechism of the bladder,
the daily questions and answers, until blood clots
clogged my drain, once a Roman fountain.
My bladder swelled as if giving birth,
then for all the world—a razor blade in the anus.
I cried "uncle". Christ and surgeon,
if you believe merely thinking it
is the same as driving in the nails,
leave my wound! Physician, heal Thyself.

SEPTEMBER 11: A FABLE

You caterpillars, who want to eat
until there is not one familiar leaf on our living tree,
in New York there are bees that will bore into your belly,
sleep with your striped velvet over their eyes,
with their feet on your heart,
that waking will eat their way out of your soft belly.
I promise you would prefer
the quick sharp beak of a crow.
Become a butterfly.

A DENTIST

I am Saddam Hussein's US Army dentist.
I flatten his tongue with a wooden tongue depressor.
His soul, the smell of his breath, rises up in my face.
I look in at the endless lung-red tunnel of corpses.
It isn't every day I have a mass murderer in my chair.
I whistle the staccato opening bars
of the overture to the *Nozze di Figaro*,
when my drill hits the nerve it plays note for note.
He gives me a look of contempt that says
I'm only a child in his entourage, a dentist,
not a torturer. I put the removable bridge
of his soul back in his mouth and tell him to rinse.
I remember, God help me, George Washington
had five slaves' teeth fixed in his bridge.

THE WATCH

See, there are two snakes copulating.
Watch long enough, like Tiresias
you will become male and female,
no longer know your mother or father.
First in your mother's belly you had a snake's heart,
then chamber by chamber you grew a human heart.
Concealed at night, you do not see the body,
but the heat around the body—the subjunctive heat
after wish and desire. In the garden at night
you cannot tell snake from human.
The theater is dark, the play is a comedy:
someone before death is begging for ten last syllables.

SONG OF AN IMAGINARY ARAB

To Edouard Roditi

Until they killed my brother who killed you,
there were readers who read and smiled at:
From the rock of my heart a horse rose
that I should ride to follow them
the night they left by taxi
from the Damascus gate and fled toward Bombay.
My heart threw me off.
If only I had robes white enough,
but my robes were full of ashes and dust.
The rouge, lipstick and eyeshadows
you left on my flesh, I washed off before prayer.
My heart was gone, it looked back at me
from a distance, its reins bitten through.

Until they killed my brother who killed you,
there were readers who read and smiled at:
It is written, man was created not from the son but a blood clot.
When I am put in the grave and those who question the dead ask me,
"Was the blood drawn from the finger of God
or the heart or His tongue?"
I will not answer. I will say, "I have heard music so beautiful
it seemed the blood of the Lord."

Until they killed my brother who killed you,
there were readers who read and smiled at:
I know there is profit in God's word, in prayer rugs, in silk and wool,
blood of the lamb and spit of the worm.
A man who rose from barber to physician,
I prize most my grandmother's brass tray, pure as the sun
without etching or design, where I first saw the angel of mathematics,
the stateless angel of astronomy.

Until they killed my brother who killed you,
there were readers who read and smiled at:
Let an old Palestinian grandmother sit in the sun
beside an old Jewish grandmother; I'll bring them sage tea,
which in Hebrew is called something like "Miriam," because
when Mary was pregnant with Jesus sage tea comforted her.
The Jew said, "Respect is more important than the Talmud."

Until they killed my brother who killed you,
there were readers who read and smiled at:
I was admiring the girl on the balcony in Gaza City
when the shrapnel hit me in the head. I did not have time
to make the break between my thought and the attack on my head.
I thought it was a flower pot that fell off the balcony.
"Allahu akhbar!" I shouted. Someday the horse will fly.

Until they killed my brother who killed you,
there were readers who read and smiled at:
Love now is more dangerous than hate.

THE OLDEST BROTHER

After P.A. Cuadra

Maria, sister, the story is—
it was the end of days.
Everything collapsed and we were left
in the street with what we wore,
twelve brothers and sisters trembling
and Mama wanting to put her arms around each of us.
At that moment, we were suffocating in the dust, listening
to the death rattle of the world.
At that moment I was thinking "Papa,"
you understand, you already know
the ways of our father,
"I'm going to look for him," I said,
my poor mother screaming,
the brothers and sisters weeping.
But what can you do when everything falls,
when time succumbs, what remains
except looking for your father?
How often we said to him "Father,
charity begins at home."
He, you know, always in the clouds,
always giving to everyone,
but demanding of us.
I ran through those black streets
while the whole city rose up
in dust and lamentation.
The shadows threw stones at me.
I felt rage, the deaf rage of a son
against a father
who abandons him,
and I blamed him

as if he were the author of Tenebrae,
the fist of destruction.
It may be—I thought—he's helping others. And so it was.
Do you remember Juan,
the caretaker? Remember
Juan, the one who left him with all the work in the field
and ran off with a prostitute?
I came across our father with his hands bleeding
rescuing Juan,
I saw him carrying Juan.
He looked at me with his gentle eyes: "Help me!"
he said. I should have shouted
"Father, Father,
why have you abandoned us?"
It's useless! You know how he is,
he always
abandons the flock
for a lost sheep.

FOR VIRGINIA ON HER 90TH BIRTHDAY

I know that at 90 sometimes it aches to sing
or to sit in a chair, that words, music, love and poetry
sometimes trip over each other.
Teach me to walk untrippingly past the grave,
to do the funny dance of the good long life.
It's easy as one, two, three. But what is one,
how is two, and where is three?
A good death is like a black butterfly
born too soon during a mild winter.

AN AMERICAN HERO

It wasn't all smell of Adirondack lilac
and flowering chestnut trees along Broadway
in the spring of 1824.
Human sewers, mostly Negroes, carried waste in tubs
at night to the Hudson and East Rivers. James Hewlett,
said to be ex-slave, ex-tubman, self-purchaser,
ex-houseboy to English actors, leapt up like a wildcat,
then like a witch, he joined a Shakespeare theater of ex-slaves,
billed himself: "Vocalist and Shakespeare's Proud Representative."
I pick his pocket.
He played Richard the Third and Othello,
sang *Il Barbieri*, *La Marseillaise*, and "O!
say not that woman's love is bought" in one evening.
Humped in silk, Mr. Hewlett called out:
"Now is the winter of our discontent
made glorious summer by this son of New York,"
to black applause. Whatever the beauty of the season,
his actors and actresses were beaten up,
his theater finally burned to the ground, speechless.

I pick his pocket.

Adrift in an open boat, he let the winds of eloquence
take him where they would. Often, late at night, he recited
speeches from Shakespeare in the street,
sometimes in the snow.
In disgrace for marrying a pretty-as-a-picture white woman,
he served six months for stealing wine, then three years
for stealing a silver watch from the vest pocket
of a dead man, a showoff laid out in tails.
What good is a watch in the grave?

He answered the sentencing with
"I have done the state some service, and they know it."
I pick his pocket.

While he was away playing with himself,
better people attended the fashionable theater
and minstrel shows, danced the cotillion. The industrious poor—
slaves who bought their freedom, or whose fathers or mothers
had bought their freedom, a few simply freed—
dressed up as no one had dressed before, hired ballrooms,
danced the cotillion too, held a benefit dance and supper
to support Greek freedom. Late in the evening,
sweating and full of whiskey, their loins sweetened,
they fell to what whites called "crazy dancing
and senseless music" that "frightened the horses."

Out, Hewlett gave one last performance, a newspaper reported:
"to great applause he made a fine speech before the curtain,
which ended up—he could not help himself—
in some kind of talk you had to be a nigger to understand."
I pick his pocket.

Signed up on a crew of freemen and slaves
he made his way to Trinidad,
"Shakespeare's Proud Representative" found a stage,
portrayed Mr. Keene playing nine tragic roles.
Sometimes he gave himself laughing gas to please the crowd
or pretended to. A one-man band,
Othello sang *La Marseillaise.* I pick his pocket.

He disappeared in New York in the Forties,
the streets slave-free after 1827,
full of Negroes and Irish; older, there is no reason to think
he was kidnapped and shipped south for sale.

What had it come to beyond the gaslights
and wood fires? History as entertainment,
a stained purse I grab. I sit in the dark, listening
to a call and response, a call and response.
For no reason, beauty reports, disappears
not like early-morning birdsong in the city
but like the report of a rifle. I pick his pocket
in the third balcony of my life; segregated from myself,
I am barely a ghost in my own poem.

LETTER TO AN UNKNOWN

Five centimeters, already Chinese,
in your mother's womb, pre-intellectual,
about sixty days. Sounds can see you,
music can see you. Fu Xu your father,
I introduce you to him, he is a painter
already saving for your education, preparing
to carry you on his shoulders to museums.
Zhu Ming your mother holds you close
as it is possible to hold a being close—
rare as an Empress, Freudian Chinese therapist,
she will teach you the joys and sorrows
of writing Chinese. May you spend
many happy years washing ink from your hands.
You have made the Great Wall of China bleed.
Who am I? Something like a tree
outside your window: after you are born,
shade in summer, in winter my branches
heavy with snow will almost touch the ground,
may shelter deer, bear, and you.

ALEXANDER FU

Surrounded by a great Chinese wall of love
he is already three weeks old and has a name.
His mother combs his hair with her hand, nurses him.
Soon he will learn the tragic news: the world is not all love.
He has already begun to earn a living,
a little of his poopoo was just put in a flower pot.
The least part of him bears the seal of his Manufacturer.

ALEXANDER'S FIRST BATTLE

Now that you are looking over the edge of the world,
who will blame you for refusing to exchange
your mother's warm breast for formula and warm glass?
Will you ever again be content? There will be laughter
and music, the solace of small talk, the solace
of art or science, twelve-year-old whiskey.
You will search the earth through hard years
to find somewhere in a timeless bed, or Venice,
or God forbid in the back seat of a car,
the return of such contentment. Alexander,
fight the bottle, fight it with all your being.
I will fight at your side.

ALEXANDER FU TO STANLEY

Big fool, my ancestors understood
we live in two societies: time and that other society
with its classes and orders, which you, Mr. America,
like to think you can ascend or descend at will.
Do I, a baby,
have to tell you there are laws that are not legislated,
judges neither appointed nor elected?
You are wetting your pants to talk to me.
Did it ever cross your mind I like to be ten months old,
going on eleven? You are trying to rob me of my infancy
because I have all the time in the world, and you don't.
On this May evening passing round the world
I probably have more diapers on the shelf
than you have years to go. I wish every time I shit
you'd have another year. Now that's an honest wish,
better than blowing out candles.
(Secretly you want to learn from me.)
You say I look like a prophet. Did it ever cross your mind
I would just like to be a bore like you?
Stop thinking about the Jew, Christian, Buddhist, Taoist thing!
The Long March wasn't from Kovno to Queens.
In summa: you are old and I am young,
that's the way it should be. I have better things to think about
than are dreamt of in your post-toilet-trained world.

A RIFF FOR SIDNEY BECHET

That night in Florence,
forty-five years ago,
I heard him play
like "honey on a razor,"
he could get maple syrup
out of a white pine,
out of a sycamore,
out of an old copper beech.
I remember that summer
Michelangelo's marble
naked woman's breasts,
reclining Dawn's nipples—
exactly like the flesh I ached for.
How could Dawn behind her clouds hurt me?
The sunrise bitch was never mine.
He brought her down. In twelve bars of burnt sugar,
she was his if he wanted her.

DARK CLOUDS

From what breast does the milk of madness course?
We know the scene
where the inside became outside: lives of the saints,
battle scenes, Calvary, an exchange of the living
for the dead, the dead for the living. On a small scale
a homeless boy makes up his address, the death
of his mother still alive, his father's suicide.
He woos a woman, feigning he's going blind,
asked what he would farm—*rifles*, he smiles.
Some believe he never learned to pray out loud
so God would hear him. Speaking to himself
as if he were the Lord, he is two persons,
three, four, five, a multitude
climbing out of the mouth of a colossal shark.
His mother's breast wept, losing its milk.
He is the nursling of dark clouds. Truth was a storm.

2002, ALAS

Where are the birthday poems
for Stalin and Hitler,
the angelhair tarts for Franco?
Where are the sweets of yesteryear,
the party hats? Our revels are not over!
They are shooting rifles in the air
for Bin Laden and Saddam.
Happy children
are making bombs of themselves
as never before.
Dreams of mass murder have only begun:
daydreams and wet dreams.
But where is the pastry?
Where are the poems?
Coming, coming, the children sing.
Coming, coming.

AN ARGUMENT

When you said that you wanted to be useful
as the days of the week, I said, "God bless you."
Then you said you would not trade our Mondays,
useful for two thousand years,
for the Seven Wonders of the ancient world.
I said, "Endless are the wonders
to which I can only say 'ah,' that our 'Ah'
who art in heaven can easily become
'ah, ah' that comforts a baby." Then you said,
"Go make a living on metaphors for 'ah,'"
that I, a lunatic, secretly want to be
the Lighthouse of Alexandria,
a fifty-storey-high collaboration
of art and science, a mirror of light
that might be seen five or ten days out to sea,
Poseidon standing on my shoulders,
the Library of Alexandria at my back,
all the wonders of Greek Africa.
I said, "Today is Monday. I want little more
than to be a hand-mirror my wife carries
in her purse with a hanky
to stop my hemorrhaging humility."

JUNE 21ST

Just when I think I am about to be tilted
on a table for death to eat—my friend arrives
playing a harmonica. It is my birthday.
He sings a little song that is a poem
written for the occasion.
How does he know the day I was born
the midwife laughed, enthusiastic
over the size of my head, chest and penis?
My mother must have told him.

My years are sheep, I shepherd them night and day,
I live with their "ba-ba."
They much prefer his harmonica to a pan-pipe.
Some years graze near me, others wander
across the valley out of sight.
I have two dogs, one dog can't do the job.
My 57th year keeps mounting my early years,
my 63rd year is giving it hard to my 57th,
my dogs are running in circles, barking for joy.

A SATYR'S COMPLAINT

It means little to me now when I am rusting away
that at dawn gods still roll out of our human beds,
that once I entered down the center aisle
at the Comédie Française, the Artemis of Ephesus
on my arm, all eyes on her rows of breasts and me.
"Who is the master of her 90 nipples?"
the public whispered. No one noticed I was in fact
a bronze satyr, my goat feet, my tail, my erect penis.
I loved confusion, chaos was paradise.
I found happiness, so to speak, on the ramps
and scaffolding of the Tower of Babel.
I danced holding a tambourine above my head
made from a brass Turkish sieve I called *time*.
Water, sacramental wine, ink once words, passed through.
In old Rome, I played the flute, but at the first sight
of my combed, perfumed, and throbbing lower half,
Lucretia thrust a dagger through her heart.
Later in Pisa, when on the Piazza a colossal
New Testament was carved in marble in Greek—
chapter and verse, I danced across Matthew, John,
Mark and Luke, leapt to Revelation, stars flashing
from my hooves. In the Basilica, virgins
lined up on their knees in white for first communion.
A proper satyr, I took half a dozen from behind.
The wafers danced on their tongues. Beautiful,
the little hearts of blood on white lace.
The Tower of Pisa leaned away from me in disgust.
I shouted back at the mob of tourists who attacked me:
You will never put out the fires of hell
with a nineteenth-century American candle snuffer.
The devil is no one, a French-Canadian plaster loon.

Frightened by my mythological smell
a bronze horse reared up, broke away
from his handler. Mares turned their hindquarters
to the north wind, bred foals without the aid of stallions.
Born for blasphemy and lust, uncircumcised half-goat,
I made my way to the Holy Land.
I am proud my bronze prick was the clapper
in many a Jewish, Christian and Moslem belle.
I must have done something right,
Jew, Christian and Moslem chased after me
throwing stones: onyx, opals, diorite,
the glass eyes of their god.
I hid in the cold lawless night of Sinai,
my companions a snail, a skeleton of an eel.
Wise man, remember every giraffe farts above your head.
What have I stolen from myself, I thought.
How can I pay myself back in kind?
The sun and moon survive absolutely without conscience.

SONG

Now there are four rivers: once there were five,
one has left without tears or a bird cry,
rivers leave their beds, have nothing else to give,
when a lover goes, love does not die—
in an empty bed love will survive.
Love, the sweet invisible spy,
is lucky: it has tears and laughter,
for a while, past, present and hereafter.

My lady's touch has a way of whispering:
"It is summer, a perfect day—cloud
after cloud." . . . The world has gone fishing.
It is right that a noisy, hungry crowd
of seagulls attacks a fluke as if it were the world.
In the lucky world, still on the wing
love whispers "it is summer, a perfect day."
May my lady's touch have its way.

THE STARTLING

When I saw the Greek hunter
painted on the fifth-century red-figured pot
was changed into a startled fawn
because he watched a goddess bathe naked,
and that his own dogs tore him to pieces,
I had already changed from myself
to another self, further apart
than man from fawn.
When coming out of my self, I woke you
in the middle of the night to carry you off
to the sea, I stopped three times
to ravish you; you took me beyond my life,
raced me from great distance to great distance,
till helpless I fell in your lap
and said I was near death.
You lifted the heavy beast's head,
still snorting and groaning, kissed me
and washed your blood from my face,
stroked me and called me "sweet one"—
then you sang your siren song,
told me how I would be remembered,
that sleep and death were brothers,
that the sirens defeated by poetry
were changed into the great boulders
on which the city of Naples,
so well known to lovers, was founded.
I kissed you and you asked gently,
since you were young and I was not,
what Dido asked Aeneas
who was soon to go to war:
"Will you leave me without a son
of your name?"

UNCERTAIN WEATHER

Uncertain weather.
The most aloof birds
come closer to the earth,
confused by the apparent
lowering of the clouds and sky.
I walk in these descending clouds.
Gulls set off.
The fish don't care.
I surf-cast a silver spoon
into the clouds
in the direction of the sea.

Last summer in Long Island
I saw a pair of white egrets
standing at the shoreline.
Now in Jamaica
I see hundreds swooping above me,
beyond Fern Gully
where the roads lead into fields of sugar cane,
the old slave plantations.

The flights of egrets remind me
of alarmed swallows—
then I see what they are doing:
hundreds of white birds
are trying to drive
a single buzzard out of the valley,
diving again and again to protect their nests.
In just a few days
I have become accustomed
to seeing egrets perched on cattle
or standing beside, motionless.

Now I see them fighting for life,
summoning whatever violence they have,
unable to be graceless.
One by one, not as a flock,
the birds dive, pursue,
do not touch.
Off the Caribbean,
a fresh afternoon wind
lifts the egrets higher
and gives the red-throated scavenger,
who must also feed its young,
a momentary passage
down into the tall moist grass.

RETURN TO ROME

Today in Rome, heading down
Michelangelo's *Spanish Steps*
under an unchanging moon,
I held on to the balustrade,
grateful for his giving me a hand.
All for love, I stumbled over the past
as if it were my own feet. Here, in my twenties,
I was lost in love and poetry. Along the Tiber,
I made up Cubist Shakespearean games.
(In writing, even in those days,
I cannot say it was popular to have "subjects"
any more than painters used sitters. But I did.)
I played with an ignorant mirror for an audience:
my self, embroiled with personae
from *Antony and Cleopatra*. Delusions of grandeur!
They were for a time my foul-weather friends—
as once I played with soldiers
on the mountainous countryside of a purple blanket.

WEDDING INVITATION

I leap high as I can for joy, higher than you think I can.
My son writes he is marrying in September in Fiesole,
I leap over my dogs, whom he invited,
although they don't understand weddings.
You, dear reader, are also invited,
after all the funerals I brought you to.
I've always been a drum major for a brass band called hope—
even when the band wasn't there. I suggest to my son
he ready his foot to break the wine glass in a white cloth
in memory of the destruction of the Temple. If he doesn't care to,
I'll leave the wine glass in white cloth around, so it may break
by happy accident. I never broke a wine glass
except when it fell off the table, or in rage. My best advice:
the usual public vows are not for nothing, when there's a problem
talk it over. I hope family history does not weigh more than
love and honorable intention. Bless you both,
now let the centaurs and Russian dancers in.

TO MY SON'S WIFE ON HER WEDDING DAY

First I embrace you. I come prepared with this,
a wedding song, a love song beneath your balcony
because the world is different now,
there is a little more hope, a wild flower of hope.
It is for you to name it.
If marriage were a canoe—a foolish idea,
most will say, marriage may be a canoe in Montana
but not in Tuscany. They are wrong. Be Iroquois.
(Let me ramble on, but remember history.)
In a canoe both paddle, see how beautiful the lake is,
in every fiery sunrise the clouds of remembrance.
Waterlilies are wild flowers. Listen to the loons
surrounded by wilderness, far from fashion.
If you ever put on war paint, jump in the lake
as soon as you can. Remember
when your brave husband caught his first fish, he wept
because he thought I would not let him throw it back.
To live together forever in one tent
you will have to learn to make fire by rubbing
two sticks together.
Iroquois know the lesson of the swans:
swans live long lives, mate for life.
In danger the very young jump on their mother's back,
she swims, carries them away. Every Iroquois prays
that a great spirit will turn the hearts of the fathers
to the children and the hearts of the children to the fathers,
lest thunder and lightning strike the earth with a curse.

THE GOOD SHEPHERD

Because he would not abandon the flock for a lost sheep
after the others had bedded down for the night,
he turned back, searched the thickets and gullies.
Later, while the flock dozed in the morning mist
he searched the pastures up ahead. Winter nearing,
our wool heavy with brambles, ropes of muddy ice,
he did not abandon the lost sheep, even when the snows came.

Still, I knew there was only a thin line
between the good shepherd and the butcher.
How many lambs had put their heads between the shepherd's knees,
closed their eyes, offering their neck to the knife?
Familiar—the quick thuds of the club doing its work.
More than once at night I saw the halo coming.
I ran like a deer and hid among rocks,
or I crawled under a bush, my heart in thorns.

During the day I lived my life in clover
watching out for the halo.
I swore on the day the good shepherd catches hold,
trying to wrestle me to the ground and bind my feet,
I will buck like a ram and bite like a wolf,
although I taste the famous blood
I will break loose! I will race under the gates of heaven,
back to the mortal fields, my flock, my stubbled grass and mud.

PSALM

God of paper and writing, God of first and last drafts,
God of dislikes, god of everyday occasions—
He is not my servant, does not work for tips.
Under the dome of the roman Pantheon
God in three persons carries a cross on his back
as an aging centaur, hands bound behind his back, carries Eros.
Chinese God of examinations: bloodwork, biopsy,
urine analysis, grant me the grade of <u>fair</u> in the study of dark holes,
<u>fair</u> in anus, self-knowledge, and the leaves of the vagina
like the pages of a book in the vision of Ezekiel.
May I also open my mouth and read the book by eating it,
swallow its meaning. My Shepherd, let me continue to just pass
in the army of the living,
keep me from the ranks of the excellent dead.
It's true I worshipped Aphrodite
who has driven me off with her slipper
after my worst ways pleased her.
I make noise for the Lord.
My Shepherd, I want, I want, I want.

A FALL (*for Stanley Kunitz*)

The mouth on his forehead is stitched and smiling,
his head is crowned with bandages,
his broken nose: Michelangelo's slave marble.
Like the last minutes of summer sunset
his cheekbones and eyes are lavender and black.
The face that hit the cement sidewalk of 12th Street
with the full force of his gravity does not frown.
I refuse to see what I know. I kiss the mouth of sorrow,
I rejoice that he is alive. I am drinking his gin
as if he were the English consul,
I a Spanish gypsy nun chased by the wind.
In his sitting room that is part-greenhouse
we are on the sea of poetry in a familiar squall.
I must speak louder now above the wind.
We are on the green and mountainous Atlantic,
yes, there is a full "cargo of roses."
Once we went through salty puddles plashing
in our brogues—the accent not our shoes. Blaaah, blaaah.
I hear the cries of poets washed overboard in my throat.
Blaaah, blaaah. It is time to hold hands and weep.
He says he is the oldest poet who ever lived,
fifteen years older than King Lear.
At Saint Vincent's I will visit his love who broke her hip.
He says, "One step closer, I might have caught her."
His walker is not dancing.
I will come Tuesday to cook, bring a new poem.
In his easy chair, his fist on the tiller, life is north northeast,
he heads windward, a hummingbird
blown out on the North Atlantic
struggling toward land to kiss a flower.

ROMANCE

I was not Eros with a limp, or sleepwalking,
even so on a December Sunday afternoon
sunning itself on a footbridge that was three planks
over a meandering dry stream,
I saw a small green snake that was perhaps a year
twist away at the first sight of me into the tall reeds
of the future—with time enough to found a nation.
I crossed the same planks, the heavy serpent
of old age oozed along behind me.
The sunlight on the bridge and the two snakes
were a sundial beyond the indications
of the world's Christian calendar.
Then I passed green fields of winter rye
already six inches high despite the early snow.
I whispered to myself:
Verde que te quiero verde. Verde viento.
Green, how I love you green. Green wind.
Child: follow the heart, follow the heart!

AN ANCIENT TALE

Among ancient trees, there stood a colossal Oak
that protected others for a thousand years.
When earthquakes leveled temples and their marble Gods,
the Sacred Oak protected the Greek countryside.
Even when lightning seized it by the throat,
it sheltered fieldworkers, orchards, nests and hives.
How many lovers had slept below its branches?
In summer, but especially in winter
when there was snow—birds and butterflies
alighted on its branches in such numbers
passing armies would lay down their weapons
surrendering, it seemed, to beauty. Profane
Criton, the Tyrant, in need of timber
for his ships and a banquet hall,
gave orders to his slaves to cut down the colossal Oak.
"This may be the tree the Goddess loves most.
It may be the Goddess herself, but its crown will fall
like any crown of a girlish king." Then Criton
killed a slave who refused to obey his command.
Taking up the axe himself, he swung in fury.
The Oak trembled, groaned, the green leaves
turned pale, then black, the tree moaned,
blood pouring out where the branches joined the trunk,
as from a bull's throat cut for sacrifice,
blood pulsing from its mouth. The Tyrant and slaves
heard a voice: "A nymph loved by Demeter,
I live in the wood; I say to all who love green,
worthless Criton will soon die—my last consolation."
Still, he struck blows at his pleasure,
till the weeping oak chained by ropes and tackles
manned by an army of whipped slaves,
fell with the roar of a great waterfall.

Butterflies, lovers, birds, snakes and rabbits,
wild cats and bears flew out of the tree
to save themselves—some without their young.
The falling giant broke the backs of a thousand trees.
Voices came from everywhere, in Greek and shrill Persian:
"We have never ploughed a field or picked a fig
without permission of the Goddess of Harvest."
"Punish this zero to the left. Punish him!"
The Goddess nodded *Yes*—the fields and forest trembled.
"I sentence him to endless Famine!" (Of course,
she could not speak to Famine because Fate
never allows the Goddesses of Harvest and Famine to meet.)
In her place, Harvest sent a messenger
saying, "Go where the earth is salt and bones,
where nothing lives but cold, pallor and fear.
Go to the screeching hag Goddess Famine.
Tell her I will put in a word for her—" the Goddess smiled,
"where it counts, if she crawls inside Criton,
hides in his body, lets nothing of the abundance I bring
give him nourishment. Take my chariot
of winged dragons to make the distance shorter."

After a wild ride beneath the amused stars,
in Scythia on a crag of the frozen Caucuses,
where the dragons could only steady the chariot
by continually beating their wings,
the messenger found Famine.
If not for a bleeding jaw and her diseased eyes,
he would not have distinguished Famine
from the pink gravel and ice around her.
Her skin so tight, so transparent, her stomach seemed a skull.
He thought Famine's throat covered with brine sang—
Famine, whose labors are always opposed
to the Goddess of Harvest, took her bargain.
She crawled the great distance to Criton

80

on three broken wings that once were elbows
to where he slept after a lusty night,
snoring away his last moments of peace,
in a purple and gold room without a household God.
Famine locked her scaled arms around him.
She blew her breath that smelled of human waste
on his face and in him, her broken teeth
stabbing his throat with the needles of endless hunger.
Then, her good work done, she turned back
from a country of cultivated fields and flowering orchards
to the fatherland she knew as home,
the mountain and valleys of bones, salt and ice.

Sleep, with its soft wings still caressed Criton,
soothed him, but now in his sleep he dreamed of feasting:
but his jaws bit into nothing, his teeth ground nothing,
his parched throat swallowed nothing.
His mouth full of sewage his tongue struggled to escape.
When he woke he said, "I am famished"
and he told the truth.
He summoned an army of servants and slaves,
ordered them to slaughter his cattle, to heap before him
meats cooked or raw, fish, fowl and frogs.
Whatever he ate, his stomach shouted in pain and anger.
He swallowed rabbits whole and turtles in their shells
and he groaned, "I am starving, I am starving."
Night and day he ate what would feed a city, a nation
but the more he wolfed down, the more he craved.
He starved as fire burns straw, crawling to dry branches,
from fallen trees to flaming forests.
Then, as an ocean eats a coastline, he hungered,
cliff by cliff, mountain by mountain,
he sucked out the marrow—all this was to him
less than a black olive, a dry fig.
His stomach was a gorge cut by a dry river.

Starving and moneyless, he called his daughter to him,
sold her for five sheep. She turned toward the sea,
crying that Poseidon had once been her lover,
hoping he would save her from slavery.
Poseidon heard her. Quick as a fish
takes to water when dropped from a fisherman's net,
he disguised her as an old fisherman,
red-eyed from the sun, skin becoming coral,
so the slavemaster did not recognize her,
saying to her simply, "Good fishing!
Fisherman, where is the slave girl I paid for?"
She answered, her voice cracked by years at sea,
"I swear, may Poseidon not watch every net
I cast if anyone has been here but me."
The fool went off with his deceived dog.
Then Poseidon's trident gave her back her own form.
Starving Criton, learning that his daughter had the power
to change her form, sold her again and sold her again
to barbarians. But she walked away,
now a mare, now a heifer, now a sheep, now a lion,
now a dove, now an eagle
till there was no food for her father to buy
till there was nothing, nothing at all—
only his own flesh for his teeth to gnaw.
He licked his fingers then ate them,
then his hands, then his wrists, then elbows,
his trotters and sex, he swallowed his own ears
and lips and tongue, portion by portion,
he consumed his own body, his whole self.

Demeter, who does not allow a field to be planted
without her permission, had made clear her will.

SATYR SONGS

A Common Satyr and poet, I want a hero
who reaches up to the matter beneath
the stanza: eight lines, ten syllables or so,
as into a lady's panties, who rhymes *breath*
and *death*, *no* if he cares to with *Galileo*,
who recanted, but fathered before his death
Natural Philosophy and three natural daughters
baptized in the Arno's muddy waters.

I cheer for *love*, what some call *vice*,
what some call *sin*, some simply pleasure,
humping, romance, odd ways of making nice,
taking advantage of, taking the measure.
One wife's passion is another's sacrifice,
one man's poison is another's cure.
A little fornication rights all wrongs,
there are no commandments in the Song of Songs.

We are made of water, earth, air, and fire
in the image of the One you-know-Who,
whose hair in the wind is Hebrew barbed wire.
On the first day when the sun was brand new,
creation a blast, He simply took a flyer,
since in darkness there was little to do,
He made us—to drown us in the ocean
of the last full measure of devotion.

Not every lady returns from the dance
with the guy who brought her, anything written
by man or woman in honest ink may rinse
away in tears. Love's not an altered kitten

in the master's lap, fed on white mice.
For every French kiss there is a France,
for every bugger there is a Britain,
for every cold hand there is a mitten.

I hate the sound of shoes, bare feet on the floor—
Mozart loved to hear the sound of hooves
on oak, marble, dirt. Köchel 44,
his concerto for woodwinds and satyr hooves,
brought "rams" to court before the Emperor.
Today you hear such music, such hooves
in Andalusian caves and orange groves,
in Greek cafés, and on the Mount of Olives.

When a boy, I first saw my lower half,
my goat hooves, my pecker, I shook in terror,
called it my old apple tree for a laugh.
How many would eat my apples to the core,
would I father a kid, a faun, a calf
as I stood helpless before the mirror,
the living proof of the Creator's error,
erotic errata, an adult who pees on the floor?

My mother told me Jesus was a satyr
so I wouldn't feel bad at Christmas without a tree,
that he worked his way through college as a waiter,
to button up my overcoat when the wind is free
(she said she'd tell me about the Devil later),
to take good care of myself, she belonged to me.
She taught me to be silly, and to be good
which brightened the night sky of my childhood.

"Live in the doghouse. It is your palace,"
she explained, "the night is now, not eternity."

I loved the Aurora Borealis.
I thought hell a city, heaven the country,
the woods, a field of wildflowers, my place.
Without cross or menorah, without poetry,
whatever the weather, I took girls at random,
one at a time, in circles, or in tandem.

The question is, how can a good and beautiful wife
live with a circumcised satyr from Queens
who thinks sin is cutting spaghetti with a knife,
childbirth the parable of the spilled beans.
To understand this mystery, this hieroglyph,
each day she needs a Rosetta Stone, she preens
burrs, hay and lice from my graying plumage,
gently combs the old madness from my rage.

Centaurs teach, satyrs are autodidacts.
I have horns, rays of light like Moses,
following the heart is my business, not facts,
lines of reason. I chase the scent of roses,
truth, meanings that fall through the cracks.
Today, Satyrs weep, suffer losses,
love after love—I pay attention to rhyme,
to sunrise and sunset, not silly-billy time.

I love all clocks that tie up time's
two legs so the Gods only hop and jump—
sure to stumble on "is" or simple rhymes
for "was." Chaos is mine, when time's a lump
I prosper, when man's undone and light climbs
back to darkness and the last swan is a hump.
I am entangled by love and untangled—
love the enchanting, love the new-fangled.

When I heard the great god Pan was dead,
I asked did he die three deaths for us: goat,
man, and God, the hand of Saturn on his head?
He taught the ways of imperfection. Devout
Pan, you died so we might know Lust instead
of moderation, so we who cannot fly can float,
drunk as you taught us, our giddy feet unsure,
walking the clouds above our moral pasture.

The trick was not to know myself, I was not
human, so I could only pretend to be
wherever I was, not a fish out of water, a Scot
in Scotland, an American shark in the human sea.
I was a word, a well-written sentence, not
a blot on the human page, not poetry,
a satyr, a freak of nature, a growth,
a knot on a tree, a goat of my word, an oath.

I said, "I will never forget you, dear,"
but what is my never, never, never worth?
Once my "never" was worth fifty years;
you could take it to the bank, a piece of earth
you could mortgage. Now my life is in arrears,
it is late December, there is a dearth
of everything, years, months, days are hostile—
I will remember you, love, a little while.

My lady's touch has a way of whispering:
"It is summer, a perfect day—cloud
after cloud." . . . The world has gone fishing.
It is right that a noisy, hungry crowd
of seagulls attacks a fluke as if it were the world.
In the lucky world, still on the wing
love whispers "it is summer, a perfect day."
May my lady's touch have its way.

PHAETON

Idle reader, one day Helios the Sun God,
the God of Fire, was shining in his palace in heaven.
The Years, Seasons, Months and Hours were singing
in the great chorus of time. News reached the God
as an echo, sounds of war, prayer,
the distant traffic of the world sometimes does.
A handsome boy was approaching in a wooden chariot,
in danger of catching fire. The boy had passed through
India and Ethiopia asking anyone old enough to be wise:
"Can the Sun God be my father?"
School friends had made fun of the fatherless boy,
although his mother Clymene explained
she had by chance met the Sun God in an orchard.
She said "I love you because you make the flowers bloom."
She said that Helios laughed with such a hoot and roar
early spring became summer in an hour. "The Sun
bit into me and the orchard—as if we were a single apple,
and you were born."

Dropping naked Spring, a real beauty, from his arms
the God of Fire turned his face away,
which allowed Phaeton's chariot to arrive at the palace
barely singed. The father got off his throne,
met his son at the flaming doorway.
"Before you ask, I tell you, Phaeton,
what your mother told you is true. You are my son."
The God could not fail to notice the boy's hair
was flaming red and burnished gold.
He had his father's sunrise.
His mother's son, he reproached his father, a God:
"Where were you when I needed you, when I was cold,
when I didn't know star from star, marble from limestone?

87

Prove you are my father!" The God replied,
"First I don't like my word questioned, sunny.
On the River Styx, on whom the Gods take their oaths,
I swear, ask me any favor—I will grant it.
Phaeton, boy chick, to celebrate this moment,
I am stocking the northern lakes with sunfish."
Phaeton smiled. "What I ask is your chariot.
The right to drive the winged horses for a day—
the chariot with the gold axle, the pulpit with gold wheels
and silver-spoked tires, crysallite and jeweled yokes."
The Sun God answered, "Gods can do what they like—
but no God takes my place in the chariot of fire—
not even Zeus has the hands for it or knowledge
of the way. In the morning, the road is up straight
to the highest heavens. The vault of heaven spins
around, drawing along the unruly stars, spinning
in the opposite direction. Horses breathing fire
relish opposing winds, their bridles clanging
across the heavens like the bells of a cathedral
one day will." The boy said, "I want the chariot."
Helios flamed, "There is an enormous form in the sky,
half man, half serpent. Its head bangs the stars
and his arms extend from midnight to noon.
From its human head hang fifty serpents' heads,
among them the heads of mortals
who never found a place in their own time,
waiting their chance. Worse, from within the creature
the terrified screams of thousands of unknown
and half-formed beings babble languages Gods detest.
The horses without my sovereignty will panic,
break their diamond-studded reins you hanker for.
This terrible form would become the master of creation
if Zeus did not spike him and hold him at bay
from time to time."

Helios threw open the gates of morning:
the nimble Hours brought the four winged horses
out of the silver stables.
They were already testing their wings and rearing up.
"Father, I hold you to your word." The Sun God nodded.
"You had my oath. But if you take my chariot,
take my best advice with it: spare the whip.
Whips and floods teach nothing.
Since the dawn of time that I am,
no horse, dog or boy learned from punishment.
Show the way clearly with a tight rein and a kind shout.
Be the Morning, Afternoon and early Evening
slant westerly. The true road lies between
yesterday, Africa and the moral north.
Follow my wheel tracks, keep one eye on the highest heavens,
the other on Death Valley. Take the middle way:
pyramids on your left, writhing serpent on your right.
There, I can almost see the eyes and mouth of departing night.
My sister, the moon, is pale as a dove.
Go quickly, boy. Be a bright dawn, a new day.
There are worse things than being the hope of the world.
Remember the cold and hungry. Do not cause a drought."
The Sun God was mumbling now, afraid of his son's fate.
The boy smiled, jumped up into the chariot.
He wished he could look his father in the eye.
He waved goodbye: "Leave the light on for me."

Dawn: Phaeton opened the dark clouds with his whip
turning them to fire, which bothered the horses.
When it was noon and the horses were high in the heavens
looking down at the oceans, one horse spotted
a herd of flying mares. In no time, the horses
were far from the usual ruts.
They knew the hand that held the reins had no authority.
The boy's mortality was light, had no history behind it,

compared to the weight of immortality.
They felt giddy. For no reason a rainbow appeared.
They answered by pulling the flaming chariot south
in a great downward bow of fire toward the mares.
Phaeton went to the whip. The four horses let off fountains
of hot urine right in the face of the demi-God.
He was playing the Sun God and he was lost in the heavens,
heading for earth. The horses smelled the mares now.
Phaeton's knees shook. He had to urinate.
He wished he never knew who his father was.
He wished his father had broken his oath.
He wished he were a bastard again. He wanted his mother.
Where is East, where is West? Who is North, who is South?
Now the monstrous serpent-human, Master of Creation
was coming toward him, and an iron eagle the size of an oak
his father had not told him about.
His aunt, the moon he had never met, was weeping.

A flaming wheel broke off, crashed into Africa and set it blazing.
All snows melted. Crete and Sicily were under water.
China was a flaming paper lantern. The great cities of the world
burned as quickly as a corn field after the harvest.
Greece and Rome were gone. The Tiber and its famous sewer
a valley of burning leaves. Every olive grove on earth,
some sacred, was either hissing embers or ashes.
The rivers that had been promised swans
in the coming summer were flaming sand.
Whatever lived on earth or in the heavens lived in terror,
at the edge of fire. The Earth Goddess called up to Zeus,
"Oh my great lover! All my harvests, all the years of laboring
good farmers I blessed, gone. The pain of the plough I bore,
the weight of milestones, the misplaced pruning hooks I suffered
come to nothing. There is not a man or woman left on earth
who is not covered in blisters. Babies are burning
in their mother's arms. My Zeus, strike down the flaming chariot,

strike down Phaeton, Helios's arrogant boy who thinks he can do
what Gods cannot do." Zeus struck the brat with a thunderbolt
and Phaeton fell to earth, an unnoticed falling star.

Helios flamed, "Zeus, you bugger, you seducer of mortal wives
and boys, disguise yourself as the great penis you are
and piss out the fires." It was dark. "To hell with you, Zeus,"
the Sun God shouted. "May you be deposed by Jews,
Christians, Muslims, Hindus, Baptists and Buddhists."
Helios wept. He took off his golden helmet.
He felt like a coal-miner in a pit.
"I see the living live by stealing fire.
I owe nothing to the world.
Since I was the Dawn of Time, I labored.
How often I found my bright work dull.
Don't you think I ever wanted to be God
of the Sea, of Music or War, come as a swan
into the bed of a Greek beauty?" Zeus answered,
"A thunderbolt is a thunderbolt is a thunderbolt . . . "
Every God and Goddess yawned. The Sun's golden tears fell
into what rivers were left on earth, making amber
that would one day become gifts between lovers,
recalled in the Song of Songs, the Canticle of Canticles.

Helios, in pity for the Earth Goddess, after a time of eclipse,
let the cooling rains fall. Eros sat on his golden shoulder.
It was time for good tempests and good blizzards.
The earth was green, there were crops and farm houses,
oil lamps and fires under soupkettles. In a blink,
mankind built marble cities and slums again.
An old Greek, not an oracle, only a clever fellow
said: "These days, you almost never see a naked swimmer—
the earth is filling with burning dumps and battle fields—
an insult to the Earth Goddess."
Altars and holy scrolls were sulfurous.

Someone shouted across the port of Athens,
"You will never crucify Apollo!"
Song-birds were all but gone.
The Greek wrote in a letter:
"The Sun can never be made to look ridiculous.
You cannot get a hook into a Leviathan,
catch him with a line, or carry him to market.
You cannot get a word out of him, or have a covenant with him.
Sooner battle the Leviathan than the Sun."

The world will never forget that when the Sun
called back his horses that had bolted, he whipped
and cursed them till the winged horses turned belly-up at his feet.
They had destroyed his son, their master, one fine day.

IN THE RAIN

There are principles I would die for,
but not to worship this God or that. To live
I'd kneel before the Egyptian insect god, the dung beetle
who rolls a ball of mud or dung across the ground
as if he were moving the solar disc or host across the sky.
I would pray to a blue scarab inlaid in lapis lazuli
suggestive of the heavens.
The Lord is many. I sit writing at the feet of a baboon god
counterfeit to counterfeit. My Lord smiles, barks and scratches,
all prayers to him are the honking of geese.
To live I'd pray to a god with the head of a crocodile
and a man's or woman's body: *our father who art in river,*
holy mother, dozing in mud, sunning thyself,
look on your young in danger, open your crocodile mouth,
the doors of your cathedral, let us all swim in.
We are gathered by the river, nesting on your tongue, swim us to safety.
Believers and unbelievers rejoice together in the rain.

About the Author

Stanley Moss was born in New York City. He was educated at Trinity College, Connecticut, and Yale University. He makes his living as a private art dealer, largely in Spanish and Italian old masters, and is the publisher and editor of The Sheep Meadow Press, a non-profit press devoted to poetry.